Chuck Baird

ACC/TPP

35 PLATES

DawnSignPress

Front Cover Photograph: ART, acrylic, 36 x 24 inches
> *As if his open palm were a canvas, the artist makes a bold, curving brushstroke through its center with the pinkie of his other hand. In this illustration of the sign for "artist," the luminous white squiggle looks like it has been poured from the small finger itself, reminding us that the artistic spark comes from within.*

Back Cover Photograph: ON THE BORDER, acrylic, 27 x 82 inches
> *From left to right, the eyes grow warmer in shading and color, alluding to the gradual change from the coldness of the hearing culture to the warmth of deaf culture.*

Producer: *Joe Dannis*
Designer: *Tina Jo Breindel*
Text: *L.K. Elion*
Editor: *Marla Hatrak*

We are most grateful to the private collectors and institutions who have kindly allowed the use of material in this book.

Printed in the United States of America.

ISBN: 0-915035-18-9

Library of Congress Catalog Card Number: 93-071138

First Printing

For more information about purchasing Chuck Baird's artwork, please contact:

DawnSignPress
9080 Activity Road - Suite A
San Diego, CA 92126
(619) 549-5330
(619) 549-2200 FAX

To Deaf children everywhere
and their hearing friends...

ACKNOWLEDGEMENTS

Many people and places have played an important role in making me the man and the artist that I am today. I would like to thank them in print for all the world to see. So let me give praise and recognition to:

My parents, *Charles and Ruth,* for their love and the Christian life they gave me.

Ruth Ann, Sue, and *Liz,* my sisters, for being Deaf and bringing sign language to my home.

My brother, *John,* for introducing me to the sound of Hi–Fi and non-traditional music.

The *Kansas School for the Deaf* for my education and social growth and for the outstanding leadership of its late superintendent, *Stanley Roth,* who gave us many valued Deaf role models as well as good teachers, both Deaf and hearing.

The Boy Scouts for its rugged life, athletic programs, and coaches, which made me a strong man and helped me to confront and overcome obstacles.

Grace Bilger for teaching me art and encouraging me to become an artist.

Gallaudet University for broadening my Deaf horizons and giving me a higher education before I transferred to the National Technical Institute for the Deaf (NTID).

NTID for providing a bridge to the College of Fine Arts at the Rochester Institute of Technology. I also want to thank *Tom Raco* and the faculty for their support and for steadily prodding me. *Robert Panara* showed me the poetic life and gave me the theatre bug. *Paul Miller* and *Bruce Sodervitch* challenged me as a painter.

Nancy Frishberg and *David Hagan* for their friendship and their confidence in me.

SPECTRUM: Focus on Deaf Artists for the inspiring and exciting years of its Deaf art colony in Austin, Texas.

The National Theatre of the Deaf for giving me a tough job which led to a lot of professional and personal growth as an artist.

The *Phoenix Day School for the Deaf* and the *California School for the Deaf in Fremont* for inviting me to work as an artist with their students.

Colleagues such as *Paul Johnston, Guy Wonder,* the late *Harry R. Williams,* the late *Frank Allen Paul, Ann Silver, Rob Roth, Betty Miller, Debbie Sonnenstrahl,* and *Tom Willard* for sharing their dreams and their faith in Deaf art while waiting patiently for me to become a full-time painter again.

Joe Dannis and the *DawnSignPress staff* for bringing me back to the real life of a painter.

The *lovers* and *buyers* of my artwork for lending my early works to be printed in this book.

San Diegans for welcoming me and letting me be a part of this city.

Last, but most importantly, to all of my friends for making life worthwhile.

- C.B.

PREFACE

This book arose from a long time dream of mine, shared with friends and colleagues, to publish Deaf art. Deaf art is a relatively new genre – an exciting and promising one. Over the last twenty years, with the increased interest in American Sign Language (ASL), curiosity about Deaf culture has grown, and so has Deaf people's pride in it. As a Deaf publisher, I have a mission to preserve our Deaf heritage for this generation and the next. It is no accident that Chuck Baird chose to dedicate this coffee-table book to Deaf children everywhere. His art, with its playfulness and wit, has a natural appeal to the young. On Chuck's canvases, ASL becomes an invitation to frolic and rejoice. It is a message hard to resist.

I was fortunate to have tracked Chuck down at just around the time that I wanted to make Deaf art available to our readers. Somewhere over DawnSignPress' offices hover the bright spirits of Frank Allen Paul and Harry R. Williams, two fine and much missed artists who played an important part in my plans for a Deaf art series. Both would, I am sure, be delighted that Chuck is leading off our very first edition of Deaf art.

I hope that students of art find that their understanding of ASL and Deaf culture is enriched by looking at and discussing Chuck's work. In addition, his creations can be enjoyed as just plain art. If this book can ignite the imagination of even one deaf – or Deaf * – child, then it will have accomplished one of its purposes. It is not too much to hope that hearing parents might own a copy and open their minds a little wider to the possibilities for their deaf children. And other hearing parents, who have already resolved that their children can be happily Deaf, will especially enjoy adding *Chuck Baird* to their coffee tables.

May this book serve as an inspiration to our readers, be they hearing, deaf or Deaf. And this is just the beginning.

Joe Dannis, Publisher

* Note: Deaf indicates membership in Deaf culture.

FOREWORD

Why do artists create works of art? Why do they have this burning desire to put their images on paper, canvas, wood, and other related materials?

"Making" art is not new. Historians tell us that art has been appreciated since the dawn of civilization. We never cease to marvel at the world's first visual paintings: cave paintings which had their beginnings approximately 20,000 years ago. The animal paintings are remarkably realistic and executed without the aid of modern painting instruments. The hunters/cave dwellers were faced with incredible odds of survival, yet they took the time to create works of art. Why? Was it for a utilitarian purpose or an aesthetic function? For instance, necklaces made of animal teeth were arranged in an orderly fashion demonstrating the need to create something "beautiful." Even working tools such as spear heads evolved from irregular to symmetrical shapes. Repeatedly, we are faced with the question, why the appetite to create art?

Whether we realize it or not, it is problematic, perhaps impossible to separate art from the "everyday" world. Whether one buys a new car or a chair or a piece of clothing, one is concerned not only with the function, but also with the aesthetic aspect. Does the car look as good as the way it runs? Is the chair as comfortable as it is pretty? Simply put, art is everywhere. Life without visual images is unimaginable.

Visual art serves two purposes: utilitarian and aesthetic. Utilitarian art objects include pitchers, chairs, or any objects which serve a special need. Aesthetic art amuses and educates the eye. Aesthetic artists have this craving to take up a brush and to interpret the world as seen through their eyes. They are brave, unselfish, curious, and conscious people as they are willing to unleash their souls for all of us to see, learn from, and enjoy. They do not hide from us. Art reflects our experiences and our positions in the society. Many of us do not have the courage to share our perceptions or interpretations for fear of being ridiculed. Yet, artists belong to this special group of people who are not afraid to share themselves with the world. This is the world of genuine artists, and Chuck Baird belongs to it.

Why does Chuck Baird create art? Does he want to create "beautiful" things or does he want to make a statement? Leslie Elion has outlined Baird's childhood, his external influences, his frustrations, and his goals in this fascinating book. Through Leslie Elion's excellent account of Baird's story, we step into his shoes and retrace his life and development.

In our age with its strong militant overtones, it is refreshing to see the wit, humor, cleverness, and gentleness in Baird's art. The humor does not "take us by storm," but rather by a soft, subtle way that is ambiguous until we "catch" the signals. His deafness is evident in his art, yet it is presented in a tranquil and benign manner. His art makes us think, analyze, inspect, and examine a deaf individual's approach to life. The ability to do so is a rare skill. You be the judge of the question: "Why does Chuck Baird create his art?"

Chuck Baird could not have appeared at a better time; a timely book, indeed! There has been a plethora of "deaf accomplishments" in this decade. A deaf president has been appointed at Gallaudet University; there has been an increase in deaf school board members; we have witnessed the acceptance of American Sign Language (ASL) as a language in its own right, the recognition of deaf culture, and improved technology to serve the needs of deaf people. This book verifies that deaf artists are a part of life and of the world. Art history books have Giotto, Leonardo, Michelangelo, and we have Chuck Baird. Whereas it is not the first book on a deaf artist (deaf artists, Goya, Prendergast, Redmond, and others have books published about them), it is the first book on a DeVia artist. A DeVia artist is a deaf artist who makes a statement in his art pertaining to his deaf experiences and perceptions. *Chuck Baird* is a milestone in the publication of art books.

Deborah M. Sonnenstrahl, Ph.D.
Chair, Art Department
Gallaudet University
Washington, DC
March, 1993

INTRODUCTION

*Painting is only a bridge linking the
painter's mind with that of the viewer.*
Eugène Delacroix

Chuck Baird, whose works are brought together for the first
time in this collection, has a large and enthusiastic Deaf
following. Outside of the Deaf community, his paintings
are mostly unknown to collectors and art lovers. Yet one
does not need to be Deaf to like a Baird, any more than one needs to
be African-American to like a Romare Bearden. For viewers who are
eager to go deeper into cultural symbols, Baird's art offers a challenge.
In many of his canvases, hands are arrested and arranged in shapes that
must be more than elaborate gestures. They are. This is Deaf art, and
Baird is among the most imaginative of Deaf artists. Those who know
next to nothing about American Sign Language and the experience of
being Deaf in the dominant hearing culture are given a glimpse of a
language and a community that are both underappreciated and
misunderstood.

Baird's use of Deaf themes and sign language motifs is only a part
of his artistic range. Understandably, he wants to be known for his skill
with various media and subjects. Still, it is his mastery of Deaf art that
sets his canvases apart and makes them new, mystifying, even
disturbing, to outsiders. Native users of American Sign Language have
reacted to Baird's displays and exhibits by freezing in their tracks,
peering in shock, joy, and disbelief – a slice of our life is hanging on
that wall. What a moment of discovery!

Born Deaf in Kansas City, Missouri, in 1947, Charles Crawford
"Chuck" Baird is the youngest of five children. Three older sisters –
Ruth Ann, Sue, and Liz – are also Deaf. An older brother, John, an
abstract photographer, is the only hearing sibling. Though his hearing
parents did not sign much and his sisters were away at the Kansas

School for the Deaf, Baird early formed a strong sense of Deaf identity. In that sense, he was blessed.

Some deaf children, like Baird, are destined to be Deaf. In the past decade or so, Deaf with a capital 'D' has come to proudly refer to users of American Sign Language (ASL) and members of the Deaf community. Children who start out as 'deaf' often grow up bewildered, unable to communicate comfortably – if at all – with their families. Despite the treatments and methods like cochlear implants, speech training, auditory training, and lipreading lessons tried on them, only a tiny minority of these prelingually deaf children learn the ways of hearing society. The rest, locked in intellectual darkness, thirsting for knowledge and communication, resemble Truffaut's wild child in his film, *L'Enfant Sauvage*, based on Harlan Lane's landmark study, *The Wild Boy of Aveyron*. Those who become successful oralists are mere carbon copies of hearing people. They make a choice as young adults to remain deaf or to convert to Deaf. Gnawed by a feeling of emptiness, tired of accommodating rather than being accommodated, many go looking for answers. And to their joy, they find it in ASL and the Deaf community. One never hears about native users of ASL abandoning the Deaf community for the wonders of oralism.

With three Deaf sisters and ASL already established at home for natural and easy communication, Baird was spared being an outsider. Genetically, too, he was extremely lucky. Artistic talent ran in his family.

At the Kansas School for the Deaf (KSD), Baird had to live up to his sisters' outstanding record in art. He did. Teachers were impressed by the maturity of perspective and detail in his drawings. Rapt in art, he paid little attention during the dreary speech lessons that were a part of the curriculum of every school for the deaf. Often scolded, he was sent to stand in a corner of the room. He made his punishment bearable by gazing at the pictures and objects all around him.

Baird did not go visually hungry. One of the KSD's art teachers was Grace Bilger, a noted watercolorist. Bilger taught him watercolor techniques and took his class to sketch the countryside and old houses.

She also arranged tours of nearby art museums, the Kansas City Art Institute and the University of Kansas' Art Department. It was then, Baird recalls, that he became hooked: nothing but painting would make him happy.

Proof of his promise came early. The first painting he submitted, at thirteen, to the Scholastic Magazine Art Contest beat out other regional entries. Sent to New York two years later, this oil rendering of a two-story, pink house covered with snow took the National Scholastic Art Award. In the five years until he graduated, Baird won gold keys in the regional competition and became a finalist for the national award in the categories of oil, watercolor, and drawing.

First painting submitted to the Scholastic Magazine Art Contest

After high school, Baird was ready to leave Kansas behind him. At just about the time that he sent in his application to Gallaudet College (now Gallaudet University), David Hays, who later became the Executive Director of the National Theatre of the Deaf (NTD), was looking for two young Deaf painters to serve as apprentice scenic artists at Lincoln Center in New York City. Baird applied and was accepted. Then word arrived from Gallaudet: he had been admitted. Feeling unready for the adjustment from midwestern life to the big city, he thanked Hays and packed his bags for Gallaudet. Hays would later summon him again and again, as if fate had a hand in steering Baird toward the theatre.

Baird was at Gallaudet for only two years. A recruiter told him about the National Technical Institute for the Deaf (NTID), a college of Rochester Institute of Technology (RIT) in Rochester, New York. Just established by a government grant, NTID was designed to train deaf students in the technical arts. RIT department majors were given support services such as sign language interpreters and government grants. The portfolio Baird had used for the Lincoln Center job got him admitted to RIT's School of Art and Design.

Though he knew choosing fine art over commercial art was risky, Baird could not see himself working for one of the major companies – Kodak and Xerox were two – in the area. Even in the early days, RIT's deaf graduates were among the best-trained applicants for hot jobs in big advertising companies in New York and Los Angeles. Still, Baird resisted. As he later said, he was convinced he was "not a fit candidate" for a career in applied art. It was too commercial and mechanical. One's heart, soul, and vision were signed over to the company in exchange for security and a regular paycheck. To Baird, this was too high a price to pay. He was more interested in filling his soul than in filling his bank account.

The School of Art and Design sprang some surprises on him. If he had imagined that his earlier successes would automatically be followed by praise in the college classroom, he was wrong. Professors and classmates criticized him for a style that lacked substance or depth. They advised him to consider changing his field. Shaken, Baird took a closer look at his work, observing some years later, "I was not really a creative or a serious artist, but only a copying machine or a camera without guts."

Ever resourceful, he made this painful awakening work for him. He began to paint every chance he got, digging deeper and deeper below the surface. Repeated experimentation worked. By the time he got his diploma, in 1974, with a B.F.A. degree in Studio Painting, no one was suggesting that he fold up his easel and go back to Kansas City.

Hoping to paint and needing money, Baird took a series of jobs in state schools for the deaf. He worked at the New York State School for the Deaf in Rome, New York, for one year. Exhausted by the demands of the job and by the "I can't" mentality of many of his students who were neglected by the previous teachers, he was unable to do any painting of his own. He then served as an artist-in-residence at the Margaret Sterck School for the Hearing Impaired in Delaware. He kept an eye out for other opportunities, but nothing surfaced.

Baird faced the depressing drawbacks of life as a fine artist. No well-to-do patrons or benefactors offered to commission his paintings, and even if they existed, his deafness and their ignorance posed a barrier to breaking through to a life as a professional artist. Unless he could make something happen, he might become the very image of a fine arts major: a shivering figure in half-mittens, starving in an unheated garret because he had spent his last dime on a pot of paint.

But Baird was lucky. He was invited to go to Austin where his sister, Liz, and other Deaf artists had gathered to participate in and support an ambitious new non-profit organization begun in 1975, SPECTRUM: Focus on Deaf Artists. SPECTRUM was fueled by Janette Norman, an energetic hearing woman whose drive and ability prolonged its life for several years. SPECTRUM was not Norman's brainchild. The entire program was run by Deaf professionals. At one point, Norman and her board of directors sought corporate funding for a center for Deaf Visual and Performing Arts to be sited in Austin. The plans eventually fell through, but many who were there have not forgotten those exciting years.

Baird at work in his studio

The story of SPECTRUM's birth and death is sad and discouraging. It tells us much about why Deaf artists need a mother organization more than do hearing artists. And it tells us even more about the internal disputes, funding crises, and bad management that doomed such a worthy group. By 1981, SPECTRUM was out of business for good. The office containing all of its papers, paintings, slides, and photographs was padlocked. The rent went unpaid for a year. To recover its losses, the building's management seized

SPECTRUM's property and sold it off at auction. To this day, Baird does not know what happened to his portrait of SPECTRUM's key people – one of his favorites – and other works.

While it lived, SPECTRUM resembled a Deaf artist's Utopia. A list of those who took part in summer conferences and who worked for the group, as administrators or as performing or visual artists, reads like a *Who's Who* of Deaf America: Betty Miller, Dorothy Miles, Clarence Russell, Sandi Inches, Charlie McKinney, Liz Quinn, Jane Norman, Patrick Graybill, and Liz Baird. And there were others as well, too many to mention. During the second summer conference, artists congregated in offices on a small horse ranch which had been converted into a Deaf art center and a meeting place. There they debated whether there was such a thing as Deaf art, and if so, what was it?

So Austin promised for a time to be the center of a Deaf Renaissance. Baird himself was hired as a staff photographer through a Comprehensive Education and Training Act (CETA) grant. He spent most of the year renovating an old house for office, paste-up, and darkroom space. Later, he was named SPECTRUM's Visual Coordinator, responsible for defining goals and objectives and generating funds to expand programs. The part of the job he liked the best involved collecting photographs and reproductions of works by more than 300 Deaf artists across the nation. This material was the planned backbone of an archival collection and a national slide library, coupled with a clearinghouse of information and a center for organizing exhibits. When the grant that paid his salary ran out, Baird answered a summons from the National Theatre of the Deaf (NTD). In between jobs, he had done the set design for an NTD production, *The Parade*, and NTD had dangled other offers in front of him. Nor was the theatre a sudden attraction. At NTID, Baird had acted in the Drama Club under Dr. Robert Panara, appearing in *My Heart's in the Highlands*, *The Madwoman of Chaillot*, and *Rashomon*.

Fearing unemployment, Baird went for the greasepaint. He felt he could give up devoting himself to acrylics and gouache, his favorite media, for a few years of acting and set design. His involvement with the NTD was to stretch to eleven years, but they were productive and instructive ones. During that time, he did the designs for various dramas: *The Wooden Boy, The Ghost of Chastity Past, or The Incident at Sashimi Junction,* and *The Dybbuk: Between Two Worlds.*

In *King of Hearts,* Baird may have turned in his most memorable performance as an actor. In the company's 1989 adaptation of Philippe de Broca's cult film classic, Baird played the Painter, creating from start to finish scenes on white paper flats: a dinner table, a basket of fruit, a town, and a mental institution. All this took place before the audience's eyes every opening night. The stunning visual topper was his sure-handed, rapid-fire tracing of the black silhouette of warring armies, using multiple brushes attached to a rod. He then slew them with random splotches of red: Jackson Pollock with murder on his mind. Asked one reviewer, "Is Baird a painter who acts, or an actor who paints?"

Baird left the NTD in 1992. He headed west to California to take up yet another artist-in-residence post at the California School for the Deaf in Fremont. In what was to be his last performance for a while, he toured Russia with the Milwaukee Repertory Theatre's *Our Town.* When that ended, his future was a question mark. He really wanted to paint full-time since he had deferred his dream for a decade, too long for comfort. The usual obstacles stood in his way.

At the same time, Joe Dannis, the President of DawnSignPress, a Deaf-owned publishing company that produces American Sign Language (ASL) materials and Deaf culture studies, was on the lookout for a Deaf painter to produce lithographs of Deaf art. Deaf people had for years been telling Dannis that they yearned to see and buy prints featuring their language and culture. Dannis himself was a fan of Deaf art. He had started out selling t-shirts imprinted with designs by Deaf artists he commissioned. He met Chuck Baird at SPECTRUM and planted a small seed in Baird's mind – think about painting Deaf art someday. After he moved to California, Dannis met Frank Allen Paul (FAP), a sign language interpreter and illustrator, who was doing a lot of art with Deaf motifs. FAP would become a friend and colleague. Dannis had already heard about Harry Williams, but it was not until he arrived on the West Coast that he met this legendary Deaf artist.

Newport Beach, 1981: Dannis remembers the moment he saw Harry Williams' *Homage to Thomas H. Gallaudet* hanging in a gallery. They agreed that the painting would be made into a limited edition of litho prints for sale. Dannis contracted with Harry Williams, or "HW," his name sign in the Deaf Community, to do more paintings. He dreamed of someday bringing Williams aboard the publishing company that was at the time just a blueprint in his brain.

Years later, when Dannis was finally ready to commission Deaf art for DawnSignPress, both Frank Allen Paul and Harry Williams were gone. Their deaths robbed Dannis and the Deaf community of two gifted men whose lives were unfairly cut short. But Dannis was not about to give up. In the interval, a new surge of Deaf pride was changing the way Deaf people saw themselves.

This late awakening grew out of the recognition of ASL by linguists as an authentic, complex language, not the bastardized English it had long been thought to be. Next came the Deaf President Now protest at Gallaudet University, begun when the board of trustees picked Dr. Elisabeth Zinser, who was not Deaf and did not know sign, to become the school's new president. The board's refusal to listen to the Deaf community's wishes sparked a revolt. For one week, student protesters appeared on America's airwaves, entering the living rooms of many hearing Americans for the first time. The drama ended in the appointment of the first Deaf president in Gallaudet's 122-year history, Dr. I. King Jordan. Throughout the weeklong events, Deaf students were sending an eye-stopping message to the surprised hearing world: We Are Deaf. Watch Us Roar in Sign.

Dannis believed the time was right for Deaf art. Learning that Baird was in California, Dannis called him and suggested a match. DawnSignPress would bring Baird on board to do nothing but paint and create in the vein of Deaf art. Neither could predict what would result, but Baird would be given a license to define the genre on his own terms. It was a gamble for Dannis and a godsend for Baird.

Nine months later, this coffee-table art book is the outcome. The arrangement produced more than eighteen paintings, not all of which are reprinted in these pages. Other Baird paintings done over the years, a few of which contain Deaf themes, are included in the plates for the reader's pleasure, to show the range and variety of his skills as they evolved with time. A number of these older works also serve to remind us that Deaf artists need not always create Deaf art. The artist's Deafness may be detectable in certain emphases, exaggerations of form and anatomical parts, and vivid color values, though no conscious effort to turn out a Deaf art piece was intended. Elsewhere, the viewer may not find any clues that the artist is Deaf. Baird (and every other Deaf artist) reserves the right to exercise creative freedom, to depart from and return to Deaf themes as the spirit moves him.

Do not misread this observation. Good Deaf art deserves to be looked at, appreciated, and judged by the same type of informed standard that is brought to bear on other culturally-specific artworks. One thinks of the paintings and sculptures of African-Americans celebrating their heritage, or of attempts by women to portray the varieties of female experience. Some critics argue that art should not be classified according to race, religion, sex, national origin, or group affiliation. "Excellence has no sex," wrote the sculptor Eva Hesse. Still, it would be a mistake to dismiss or ignore differences in experience and perception. More than just the white male viewpoint demands our attention. Today, curators and art historians almost need a degree in anthropology to deal with sensibilities that were not discussed in graduate school. This lack of knowledge may partly explain why some excellent Deaf art, with a few notable exceptions, does not appear in galleries or on museum walls.

Another explanation for Deaf artists' invisibility has to do with the trouble they have in overcoming the communication barrier. In an interview, Baird ruefully remembered the one and only time he tried to hawk a line of clothes he had designed while working for

SPECTRUM in Austin. Alone one sunny Sunday, without a sign language interpreter or a hearing friend, he stood on a street corner with his homemade merchandise, looking to attract buyers. Sunday browsers passed by in a steady stream. A few who stopped to check out his wares moved on when they realized Baird was Deaf. By day's end, he had not sold a single garment. Disenchanted, he gave up.

Baird views the communication impasse between Deaf and hearing people with irony and wonderment rather than anger and frustration. His detachment can be misinterpreted as coolness. In *Deadlock*, 1989, which placed second in a juried member exhibition hosted by Deaf Artists of America, Baird fixes the white kerchief dead center in a long coil of hemp rope suspended in air. The tug-of-war may be over, or it may be about to begin. For now, there are no victors. The kerchief, hanging in limp surrender, has an aura of paralysis or defeat. One can imagine that the signal to the two teams of contestants to start pulling will never be given.

The Detour, 1992, the final plate in this book, can easily be passed over as just a scene Baird decided to paint to stay in practice: building, pavement, warning sign of construction or danger ahead. Those aware of what it is like to be Deaf in a hearing world know better: we are constantly diverted to side roads on our journeys, forced to ask for accommodations and services that are often denied us. Unlike our hearing counterparts, we cannot take for granted a direct route to our destination. The sign's bright orange contrasts to the bleak grayness of the archway into which we must venture. There are no furnishings or welcoming personnel in the chilly interior to assure us of arriving safely without getting lost in a labyrinth. That the actual model for this was a federal building in Louisville, Kentucky, is also significant. The government can be more of an enemy than a friend.

A decade of acting with the NTD inspired changes in Baird's painting style. Always a fluid performer in ASL, he noticed how his two endeavors were influencing one another: "I've noticed my signing as a storyteller has become more confident and graceful; I feel as if I paint the words in the air as though they were images on canvas. My painting skills have helped me in my work as an actor…each craft gives the other more strength."

The theatre's influence is unmistakably alive in the first painting he did for DawnSignPress' Deaf art series, *Double Nine Lives,* 1992. Full-face, a yellow-eyed cat fills out the narrow frame. The deep purple background thrusts the feline closer to the viewer. A pair of opposing hands – Baird's – on either side of the animal's face pull taut one strand each of its whiskers. This is how the sign for "nine" and "cat" are formed, though the movement and location for "nine" are different. Here Baird teases us with a visual pun set in a canvas that could form the backdrop for an NTD production. It also helps to know that the NTD troupe delights in visual puns.

Just as dramatic is the 48" x 48" *Tyger, Tyger,* 1992. Here, the outsized, looming head of the mythical tiger of William Blake's famous poem stares ferociously outward. Its eyes and stripes are fearsome. Dwarfed by its immensity, a small, moist-eyed young man sits beneath it, wearing slippers out of the *Arabian Nights.* Aladdin? Unafraid, he seems to be clawing his cheeks. He is actually making the sign for "tiger." There is no ground beneath him, only a hint of a magic carpet. These small clues explain why the young man does not fear being devoured by this hellish beast: it is unreal, just an apparition.

In his early attempts to develop a style, Baird played with photorealistic techniques that were all the rage in the 1970's. He admired the ultrarealistic urban landscapes of Richard Estes, with their trapped-in-windows reflections of scenes ordinarily outside of the canvas frame. *Ski Shop,* 1982, shows how skillfully Baird pulled off optical magic. Thick, slashing white panes make a grid in the window. Our eyes, held for a moment by this forceful pattern, turn to the hemmed in, slender skis. Their bright shades and steel leggings are a soft contrast to the imprisoning whiteness. One can be fooled into believing that this is Meyer's ski shop when Meyer's is actually across the street. Beyond the window sits a yellow truck, which would seem to be parked right inside the shop if it were not for its calculated, offside placement and light refraction, achieved by diluting the pigment. It is lightly, subtly done.

The eye is also wooed by *Cornfield*, 1986, and *Santa Monica Pier*, 1987, two paintings that mark a period of dabbling in varieties of light, shade, and color. The cornfield is a wavy sea of green. It casts off a latticework of shadows which wriggle toward the end of the frame. Light radiates off the tips of the fronds and seeps into crevices. One's gaze is drawn first to the cornstalks, but inevitably, the shadows call it back and hold it fast.

Under the Santa Monica pier, the row of poles is disturbed by swirling chocolate waves topped by creamy, curling whitecaps. Above, the crazy assortment of beams parallel the churning going on below: all is disorder. The poles' long shadows recede backward to the rear of the frame, as if pushed back by the insistent tides. Worn away by pounding waves, a few of the poles have had their finish stripped to a whitewash. They now look more like the whitecapped tides they have been built to withstand. A triangular splash of green at the right bottom corner directs us to the safety of shore. More than a mere pier, more than an ocean's turbulence on a typical California afternoon.

A markedly different treatment of color and theme stands out in *Locomotive Wheels*, 1987. The white-grey wheels are perfect ovals. With their melon-shaped flaps, they are overlaid by mechanical parts that each have an exact place in the design. A tier of pneumatic piping stretches overhead. The machine could have been freshly assembled just that morning by a team of engineers determined not to let mud or dust ruin their work. Only the track's rusted rail and wisps of dried grass ruffle the train's handsome Art Deco look. One is reminded of the enormous machine in Chaplin's *Modern Times,* a flawless monument to progress until Charlie gets caught in its merciless cogs. Baird's vision of the locomotive is streamlined and sexy; so beautiful an invention should take us to where we want to go in a twinkling.

By his own admission, Baird is bewitched by color, light, and shadow. Because he is Deaf, Baird regards vision as an acute sensory gift. However, he disagrees with theorists who claim deafness results in keener powers of sight. Deaf people may compensate by growing more aware of environmental cues and body language, but deafness from birth, Baird believes, does not automatically trigger an enhanced ability to see. If it did, art schools and galleries would have long ago made a note of the unusual number of Deaf talents who were dropping off their portfolios. The Deaf community's share of painters is no greater than that of the hearing world.

While Baird's eyes may be no different from a nondeaf painter's, his perception is. Even without referring to studies showing that Deaf children who sign from early childhood develop cognitive skills not seen in hearing children the same age, we know that deafness and sign language must naturally set us apart. Baird dreams and thinks in sign; so do we. Music for hearing people is, for us, signed poems and stories. The instruments that bring joy to those who hear are sung or played; ours arise from our hands and the language they make. This language constitutes a culture which hearing people often cannot comprehend. "I'm grateful to my Deaf sisters," Baird has said. "They made me think sign language was normal." Hearing people may wonder how a sensory loss can be something to celebrate. Baird, a cultural ambassador, can tell them through his art: what may seem like a loss to be grieved is not. Deafness is not a pathological condition to Deaf people, but a different way of being. Life in a world designed for those who can hear is not a bowl of cherries, but so what? Sign language and the Deaf community would not exist without deafness. Few may be convinced, but Baird's Deaf art is a testimony to the vibrancy of a community that refuses to, in Sir Thomas Browne's words, "lie down in darkness."

Like many Deaf painters, Baird went through a phase of commenting on cultural oppression. His experiments were influenced by Dr. Betty Miller's satire, embodied by her *Bell School, 1944.* This powerful painting attacks the bondage imposed on Deaf schoolchildren who were forced to learn to speak – badly – and not allowed to sign. These children often wound up "oral failures," their education crippled because learning was neglected in favor of speech training. Baird's send-ups of the educational establishment's obsession with hearing and speech appear in *Mechanical Ear,* 1973, and *Why Me,* 1973. The mechanical ear is literally that. Giant-sized, it is stuffed with multicolored wires, gadgets, and meters, the tormenting paraphernalia Baird was hooked up to as a child. Alumni of schools for the deaf will nod. Hearing tests were a hated part of growing up Deaf.

Chuck at his easel

The body aids in *Mechanical Ear* were later replaced with behind-the-ear models, but the unhappy memories lingered. Many hearing aids now languish in drawers because their owners said "to hell with them." When they came of age, it was time to please themselves, not their hearing teachers or parents.

Why Me? also ridicules orally fixated education for Deaf children. Four identical egg-shaped heads are lined up in two rows. Look closely, and you will realize that the four heads are actually one image in a moving freeze-frame. In every ear, wires dangle down from boxy hearing aids. For eyes and foreheads, there is yellow yolk, as if the thinking mind has been replaced. And indeed it has: from left to right, each brow is inscribed with a vowel, sound, or consonant, the speech teacher's tools. (What deaf school graduate doesn't remember those boring exercises "…say 'puh.' Good, now say 'buh.' No, no, 'buh,' 'buh.' Please do not spit.") Read as a unit, the letters form the question, "Why me?" Baird cleverly spells his message "wh i̅ m e"; the pronunciation symbol takes us by surprise. Thin wires run down each mouth to the chin, suggesting marionettes controlled by an unseen hand. And depending on which consonant or vowel they try to utter, the mouths are shaped in an "O" (wh) or pursed (m). Baird's painting owes much to Miller's justifiably angry works. Because he lacks the rage over cultural and linguistic oppression needed to keep producing this type of biting satire, he soon changed direction. Baird has suffered insults and indignities at the hands of hearing people. However, he is too gentle to throw a painted Molotov cocktail at his tormentors. He is no revolutionary.

What he is, as his later works demonstrate, is a celebrant. Coming after the Miller-inspired pieces, *Hands o' Texas,* 1979, is among his first tries at arriving at something different with a Deaf theme. The painting is simple enough: the state of Texas is shown as two overlapping hands. One hand is laid down diagonally. The other hand hangs over it horizontally. Both palms face out. Each thumb overrides the opposing wrist. The topmost thumb represents El Paso and Ciudad Juarez, coming to a halt at the Rio Grande; the bottom thumb covers San Antonio, Corpus Christi, and Laredo. The lower hand's two last fingers are curved inward to avoid spilling into Mexico. A Deaf man's Texas in color pastel.

Another feature in Baird's work that makes him unmistakably Deaf is the use of double or triple identical images, like arms or heads, to show a sign in motion. This is not a new pictorial device. Since the nineteenth century, painters have known how to draw a limb in a dozen different perspectives. But it was not until the motion studies of American photographer Eadweard Muybridge (1830-1904) that many thousands of individual optical facts were finally recorded for the human eye to see. Muybridge began his experiments innocently enough when he was hired by the Governor of California, Leland Stanford, to settle a bet on whether a galloping horse ever lifts all four feet off the ground. His sequential frames, which froze the horse's stride in the blink of the camera's shutter, proved that it did. For want of a better word, this freeze-frame technique can be called "sequentialism."

The Deaf painter Frederick LaMonto used sequentialism in his *Helen Keller's Breakthrough.* Both Anne Sullivan and Helen Keller are shown with two heads to mark the passage of time. The second heads stop at the moment of revelation. Sullivan is at the water pump, holding Helen's hand (#1) under the spigot. Water gushes out. In hand #2, Helen forms the letter "W." Hands #3, 4, 5 and 6 complete the word "w-a-t-e-r." No one who looks carefully will think that LaMonto had created a grotesque, six-handed mutant wearing a frock.

Baird may not have seen LaMonto's depiction of how Helen Keller discovered language and meaning. He did not need to. A lifelong signer and an actor, he was comfortable with innovative experiments. He knew how to break signs down into slow motion to show handshape, location, movement, orientation – the four basic components of signs – in a natural flow. Such a treatment occurs in *Best Friends,* 1992. In head #1, the dog faces left, away from its master. Responding to the summons, he turns his head to the right (head #2) in a freeze frame. The two heads are attached, but there is no feeling of freakishness; the dog's movement is evident. Similarly, the owner touches his thigh – the first part of the sign for "dog" – and a second hand, lower down, has him snapping his fingers. Both hands are clearly his. By strategic placement and shadings, Baird helps the onlooker to understand that an exchange of communication has taken place.

Fingerspelling is not a Baird hallmark. Fingerspelled words have been absorbed into other paintings, notably those of Morris Broderson. Baird prefers signs themselves as a more natural expression of Deaf identity. His Deaf series for DawnSignPress makes rich use of ASL, as can be seen in *All American Breakfast,* 1992. Here, the body and spout of a syrup bottle has turned into a hand and a thumb out of which syrup pours onto a plate of pancakes. It is as if human parts have been transplanted onto an inanimate object. It is a startling union of two incompatible forms. Such a merger, this time of hand and tail, takes place in *Cetacean Blue,* 1992. Instead of a forked tail, the playful whale, traveling with its pod, is endowed with a hand breaking the ocean's surface.

Replacing objects, parts, and utensils with hands and fingers in every painting would have been boring. So Baird tried his hand at "mirroring" a subject, attaching to it an ASL alter ego. A good example is *Crocodile Dundee,* 1992. A pair of rigid, outstretched arms lie directly beneath a crocodile's terrifying jaws, parodying their drawbridge motion.

More detailed yet in the same manner, *According to Coyote,* 1992, weds the mystical to the wild. A coyote, scenting an oncoming storm, perches on a high boulder in the desert. The upper and lower halves of the painting seem to have split; a line of blue wash slicing across the center marks a change in hemisphere. Clouds billow into a mushroom cap, half of which assumes the form of a ghostly Navajo Indian signing "coyote." None of these elements was chosen by accident. Baird spent hours in the library researching Indians and coyotes. Before he lifted a brush, he had in mind the idea that the Indian worship of nature and its animals could be joined somehow to his own worship of ASL. The white man's destruction of Native American culture can be compared to hearing people's suppression of Deaf culture. Perhaps Baird didn't analyze the connection this deeply, but it isn't absurd to suggest that he considers Deaf people the Native Americans of the modern-day hearing world.

In *America's First Deaf Teacher,* 1993, Baird honored Laurent Clerc, the Deaf Frenchman who came to America in 1816 at the behest of the Reverend Thomas Hopkins Gallaudet. Clerc, who brought French Sign Language to the United States and was one of the founders of the American School for the Deaf in Hartford, Connecticut, is a hero to Deaf Americans. A movement is now underway to give him a greater share of the credit for establishing schools for the deaf in this country. Baird shows Clerc as a majestic head on a bust. A left hand, painted in flesh tones to link living Deaf Americans to the departed Clerc, touches his cheek with two fingers. This was Clerc's name sign, created because of the scar on his left cheek. The elm tree in the background is from Clerc's school for the deaf in Paris and is central to a famous story about him told by Gilbert C. Eastman in his play, *Laurent Clerc: A Profile.*

Back in 1989, Baird was approached by an arts committee established to set up exhibits and workshops at Gallaudet University for The Deaf Way. The Deaf Way was an historic event for thousands of Deaf people in the United States and abroad. Designed as a festival combining many strands of Deaf life, including education, arts, entertainment, and communication philosophy, it was a huge financial and organizational undertaking. Though it lasted only a week, its impact on the thousands of visitors who attended was profound and enduring. Gallaudet University has always been a mecca for Deaf people from all walks of life. The Deaf Way was a once-in-a-lifetime happening. And then there was Baird.

Commissioned to do a mural, Baird was handed the task of painting the Deaf Experience. The work had to have a universal reach; it would be by an American, but it would not bear a "made only for Deaf Americans" stamp. It had to speak, or sign, to every Deaf person of every nationality. And it would hang as a permanent memorial to The Deaf Way.

Finished in three months, the mural has provoked a curious range of reactions from viewers. Unlike anything Deaf artists have conceived, then or since, Baird's Deaf Experience mural had a definite narrative scheme. The mural required a lot of study and repeated viewings before many Deaf Way participants could understand its message.

Filling the panel is an array of hairless and sexless figures. They are stripped of the usual identifying human characteristics, except for eyes, ears, and noses. Even these have a strange, not entirely human appearance. Our first impression is straight out of science fiction or *Star Trek*. The bodies themselves make us pause. Muscular to an extreme, they look like Olympic champions. These creatures are all exaggerated bone, joints, sinew. For all we know, a scientific experiment in which automatons were mated to humans went horribly wrong, generating a race of mutants, half human, half robotic. No wonder Deaf viewers were disconcerted, even repelled: we're made to look like aliens.

Next, the colors fairly assault the eyes. They glow with fluorescent brightness through each figure's skin. Baird gives us an ethnic stew of many shades: green, brown, mauve, orange, olive-green, yellow, off-red, purple. Different as we are, one thing unites us all: Deafness. Race, age, sex, and nationality – none of these should matter.

Brightest of all are a pair of golden hands in the upper left corner of the first panel. The creator – Baird, of course – intended these to be worshiped by the mortals below...the sun as warming hands. American Sign Language is our sun, the radiant key to unlocking communication and letting in light and understanding. That much is clear. Roam through the crowd, and you will see, here and there, hands interlocking, making contact. An orange adult signs, "Deaf, me too," to a small yellow child, who asks, "Deaf you?" in grammatically correct ASL. A purple figure whose arms stretch through two panels points toward the source of light for others who may not know that there is hope. Throughout, hands are raised imploringly, hands touch, hands lift, hands comfort, hands love. The work could just as easily be titled *Hand Love*.

Baird painting Gallaudet University's mural

Just underneath the sun-hands, a somber brown figure gazes directly at the viewer, its hand pointing like Uncle Sam in the World War II army recruiting poster: Uncle Sam wants you! Baird has said that the finger can mean accusation, a call to arms, or a reminder. Whatever emotion it stirs in its audience should rumble in the gut and prick the conscience. The questions one might ask of oneself are intimate and private: Have I been true to myself as a Deaf person in a hearing world? Have I supported my

Deaf brothers and sisters? Have I asserted my right to be here? Do I take pride in being Deaf? What am I ashamed of? Those who carry a secret burden may stand here for some moments, lost in silent debate.

In the second panel is a pair of upflung arms belonging to someone whose face is blocked by another citizen of this planet. Fists clenched in victory, the arms are spread apart in a triumphant 'V.' Older Americans will remember this famous victory sign flashed by Britain's wartime Prime Minister, Winston Churchill. Could this refer to our Deaf Churchill, a leader who will urge us on, past blood, sweat, and tears, to vanquish the enemy? Hardly. Comparing hearing people to Nazis is just plain silly. Only the most militant Deaf activists would interpret Baird's intent so literally.

Still, 'V' is for victory, yes. A victory over ignorance, discrimination and prejudice. A victory over the legacy of the 1880 second International Congress on Education of the Deaf in Milan, Italy, an infamous page in Deaf history that has left an ugly rift between the Deaf community and hearing parents and educators. Educators in Milan did the unthinkable: they decreed that speech was to be the only communication tool in classrooms worldwide. The use of sign language was forbidden. Deaf people had no say in the decision. Slowly, Deaf teachers vanished from all schools for the deaf. Deaf children were deprived of role models and shut off from natural transmitters of ASL and Deaf culture. It took decades for qualified Deaf teachers to again appear on deaf school campuses. The war continues to this day, with those favoring the oral method on one side, and those favoring ASL on the other. For Deaf people, it is a battle for self-determination.

Baird knows his Deaf Experience mural has political overtones. The small child asking the adult, "Deaf you?" recalls the poignant story of the young boy at a school for the deaf who was asked what he wanted to be when he grew up. He replied that he could not be anything because he would die at 18. Never having seen or met a Deaf adult, he believed that all Deaf children perish before reaching maturity. How appalling! How sad!

Baird's three older Deaf sisters spared him this kind of despair and pain. A sensitive man, he knows from his encounters how tough it can be for deaf people who are not members of the Deaf community to fit into a niche. Neither hearing nor Deaf, they are stuck in limbo. The social isolation that often accompanies deafness can be devastating and can destroy the spirit. In a note to the author, Baird summed up his philosophy: "A happy life...uses both light and shadow to produce beauty. [This] applies to my life as a Deaf person; oppression can become a blessing because it forms a dark backdrop for the radiance of hope." What saves him, what saves so many of us, is the Deaf community, whose very purpose for existing is to sustain communication through a most remarkable visual medium. Through this medium a living language thrives, worthy of study by linguists, worthy of teaching and learning, and worthy of awe: American Sign Language.

Vive art! Vive Deaf art! Whether you admire him as a Deaf artist, or as an artist who happens to be Deaf, Chuck Baird has painted with passion and devotion for thirty years now, refusing to let the hardships of his profession drive him away from his great love. We are proud of his achievement, and we are pleased to share with you the fruits of his seeing eye. Take a detour, then, and turn the next page to get to know the wonderful art of Chuck Baird.

L.K. Elion
San Diego
February, 1993

BIBLIOGRAPHY

BOOKS

Arnheim, Rudolf. *To the Rescue of Art: Twenty-six Essays.* Berkeley and Los Angeles: University of California Press, 1992.

Arthur, John. *Richard Estes: The Urban Landscape.* Boston: Museum of Fine Arts, 1978.

Fairbrother, Trevor. *Robert Wilson's Vision.* Boston: Museum of Fine Arts, 1991.

Gannon, Jack R. *Deaf Heritage: A Narrative History of Deaf America.* Maryland: National Association of the Deaf, 1981.

Hall, Robert L. *Gathered Visions: Selected Works by African American Women Artists.* Washington, D.C. and London: Smithsonian Institution Press, 1992.

Hunter, Sam. *Rivers.* New York: Harry N. Abrams, Inc., 1970.

Padden, Carol. "The Deaf Community and the Culture of Deaf People." In *American Deaf Culture: An Anthology,* edited by Sherman Wilcox, 1-16. Maryland: Linstok Press, 1989.

Szarkowski, John. *Looking at Photographs: 100 Pictures from the Collection of the Museum of Modern Art.* New York: The Museum of Modern Art, 1973.

Woodward, James. *How You Gonna Get To Heaven If You Can't Talk With Jesus: On Depathologizing Deafness.* Maryland: TJ Publishers, Inc., 1982.

ARTICLES

Baird, Chuck. "My Life as an Artist." Unpublished autobiography, 1989.

Baldwin, Steve. "A Retrospect of SPECTRUM: A Hard Lesson to Learn." *The Deaf Texan* (January 1988): 9-10.

Hughes, Robert. "Telling an Inner Life." *Time* (December 28, 1992): 68-69.

Langham, Barbara. "Focus on Deaf Artists," *Exxon U.S.A.* (Second Quarter, 1980): 22-25.

Leamon, Emily. "Chuck Baird: Creating Art on Stage and Canvas." *NTID Focus* (Spring/Summer 1983): 30-31.

Roth, Robert I. "Is There a Deaf Genre?" Keynote Presentation at Deaf Artists of America Conference, Washington, D.C., July 9, 1987.

Wilding, Terry. "Masterpiece: Chuck Baird's Gallaudet Mural Captures Essence of Deaf Culture." *Deaf Artists of America Newsletter* (Fall 1989): 4-5. Reprinted with permission of *Buff and Blue*, Gallaudet University.

The author also used information from dozens of newspaper clippings, press releases, and the National Theatre of the Deaf materials which Chuck Baird generously made available to her.

Chuck Baird

35 PLATES

SUNSET, 1984
Acrylic, 23 x 18 inches
Aaron B. Weir, Ohio
Palm trees stand like sentries as the sky darkens in soft blue-pink ripples.

Opposite: ALL AMERICAN BREAKFAST, 1992
Acrylic, 34 x 28 inches
The body and spout of a syrup bottle metamorphoses into a hand and a thumb out of which syrup cascades onto a stack of pancakes.

Below: SKI SHOP, 1982
Acrylic, 16 x 20 inches
C. Robert Ohman, Jr., Connecticut
This painting dates from Baird's photorealistic period when he experimented with window reflections and optical illusions.

Chuck Beard '92 ®

Opposite: VIEW OF CHESTER from Bonfanti's office, 1987
Pencil, 12 x 40 inches
Billie Bonfanti, Connecticut

VIEW OF CHESTER from the hill, 1987
Pencil, 12 x 40 inches
Billie Bonfanti, Connecticut
During his time with the National Theatre of the Deaf (NTD), Baird often drew the landscape around the New England town in which NTD was headquartered.

Below: CORNFIELD, 1986
Acrylic, 22 x 28 inches
SPRINT, California Relay Service
Baird's backyard looks like a scene from an Iowa farm at harvest time.

Opposite: WHY ME?, 1973
Acrylic, 26 x 26 inches
Nancy Frishberg, California
This question is posed by four egg-shaped heads that each have mouths controlled by wires, the artist's biting commentary on the sorry state of the education of deaf children.

Below: THE MECHANICAL EAR, 1973
Acrylic, 30 x 30 inches
Paul Johnston, Maryland
A giant ear is festooned with dripping wires, meters, and gadgets, all the dreaded instruments that every deaf child learns to endure, then reject in adulthood.

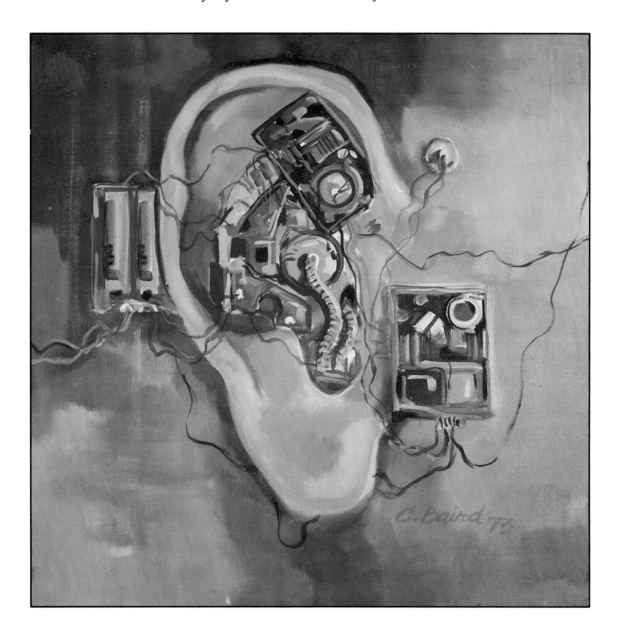

Opposite: BEST FRIENDS, 1992
Acrylic, 28 x 48 inches
In response to his master's snapped finger, a dog turns its head in a
double-movement effect.

Below: DOUBLE NINE LIVES, 1992
Acrylic, 24 x 48 inches
A pair of opposing hands pull taut one strand each of a glow-eyed cat's whiskers,
forming the sign for "nine" and "cat" simultaneously.

Opposite: LOCOMOTIVE WHEELS, 1987
Acrylic, 24 x 30 inches
Susan Baird Gordon, Kansas
All spit and polish, these stylish Art Deco wheels make a locomotive look like a travelling display of art.

Below: THE CAMERA, 1979
Acrylic, 23 x 29 inches
Donald E. Bangs, Maryland
A camera's parts punctuate the canvas in a carefully choreographed kaleidoscope of color.

Opposite: SUMMER PALACE in Beijing, 1987
Acrylic, 20 x 15 inches
Aaron B. Weir, Ohio
Painted during an NTD tour of China.

A FLOWER STALL in St. Gallen, Switzerland, 1982
Acrylic, 16 x 22 inches
From the permanent collection of the National Technical Institute for the Deaf,
a college of Rochester Institute of Technology.
*Flowers, here and abroad, appeal to Baird's sensual eye and remain one of his favorite
still-life subjects.*

Below: SANTA MONICA PIER, 1987
Acrylic, 18 x 24 inches
Collection of Deaf Artists of America, New York
*Convulsive waves, jumbled beams, a sun-lit California shore — chaos and order are
both found beneath the pier.*

Opposite: BLACK TIE ONLY, 1992
Acrylic, 38 x 30 inches
A flock of penguins afloat on a frozen archipelago surround one human figure in black tie and tails.

Below: CARUNCLE, 1992
Acrylic, 22 x 28 inches
The soft folds of a turkey's neck are counterportrayed by a kneeling female model, depicting 'gobbler' in ASL. The model's fingers are made out of wood and are designed to be swung in an imitation of a caruncle, better known as wattles.

UNTITLED, 1989
Acrylic, 120 x 360 inches
Gallaudet University, Washington, D.C.
The Deaf Experience in five panels, commissioned by Gallaudet University for The Deaf Way celebration. It now hangs permanently in the University's cafeteria.

Opposite: WHOOO'S THERE?, 1992
Acrylic 28 x 34 inches
The yellow eyes of an owl double as binoculars through which a birdwatcher peers.

Below: FINGERSHELL, 1992
Acrylic, 24 x 36 inches
A man's hand, in playful and gentle mimicry, joins a brood of turtles as they amble onto a pebbled path.

Below: COLORS #1, 1993
Acrylic, 20 x 40 inches
Signing 'color,' a model's outspread hand, with each finger a different shade, is held to her
mouth. Soft pastel swirls in the dark background complete the effect.

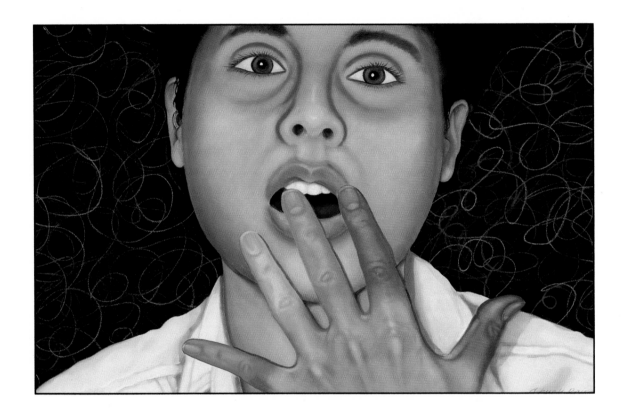

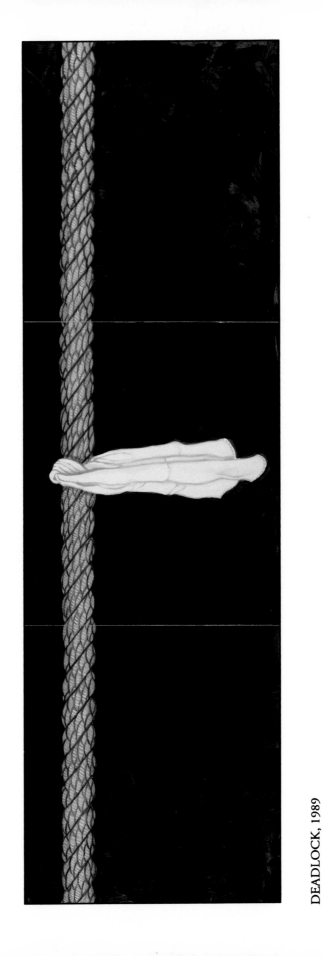

DEADLOCK, 1989
Acrylic, 28 x 84 inches
The communication impasse between deaf and hearing people is portrayed by a game of tug-of-war in which there are no obvious victors.

BLUE HENS
Acrylic, 18 x 24 inches
From the permanent collection of the National Technical Institute for the Deaf,
a college of Rochester Institute of Technology.
Brilliantly blue, these hens appear to be the wondrous result of a cross-breeding
experiment between species of different colors.

CETACEAN BLUE, 1992
Acrylic, 30 x 60 inches
*A fish and a pod of whales cavort; two tails shaped like human hands break the
surface, one forming the sign for "fish," the other, for "whale."*

Opposite: IF I WERE M.C. ESCHER, 1993
                   Pencil, 13 x 15 inches
                   In a tongue-in-cheek homage to the self-referential, image-within-an-image
                   illustrations of M.C. Escher, two diametrically opposed hands make the sign for 'artist.'

Below: HANDS O' TEXAS, 1979
                   Color pencil, 12 x 18 inches
                   Texas Commission for the Deaf and Hearing Impaired, Texas
                   The borders and contours of the State of Texas are shaped by two overlapping hands.

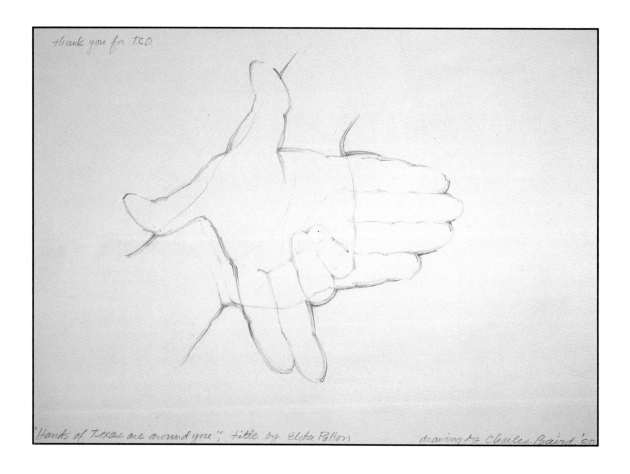

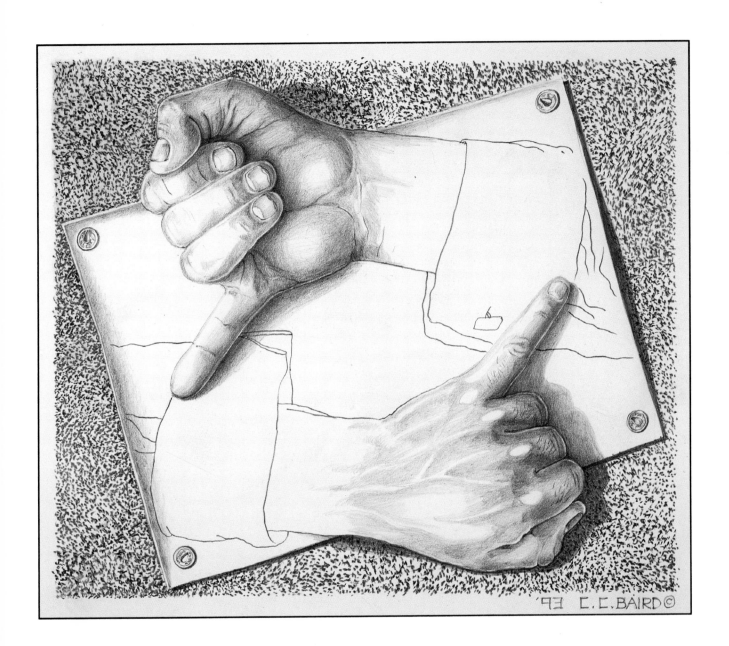

'93 C.C.BAIRD ©

Opposite: TYGER, TYGER, 1992
Acrylic, 48 x 48 inches
The looming visage of Blake's mythical Bengal tiger stares ferociously outward, seemingly engulfing the cross-legged, moist-eyed figure at its base bravely signing, "Tiger."

Below: ACCORDING TO COYOTE, 1992
Acrylic, 24 x 30 inches
Scenting an oncoming storm, a coyote perches on high ground in the desert as a cumulus cloud, transmogrified into a Navajo Indian, mushrooms overhead.

Opposite: AMERICA'S FIRST DEAF TEACHER, 1993
Mixed media, 40 x 30 inches
Laurent Clerc, the Deaf Frenchman who came to America in 1816 at the behest of the Reverend Thomas Hopkins Gallaudet, is honored here. The elm tree in the background is from Clerc's school for the deaf in Paris. It is central to a famous story about him told by Gilbert C. Eastman in his play, Laurent Clerc: A Profile.

Below: MY SUPT., 1993
Acrylic, 29 x 21 inches
An affectionate tribute through architecture rather than portraiture, this painting of the Kansas School for the Deaf's Stanley D. Roth Administration building, with its plays on light and shadow and its simple plaque, is a reminder of the lasting influence of one superintendent (known as "Supt." in ASL) of a school for the deaf.

THE DETOUR, 1992
Acrylic, 21 x 29 inches
*A symbolic passageway is blocked by a sign that says 'Detour,' forcing unseen
pedestrians to enter a forbidding, high-vaulted building where one can easily get
lost: the route drawn for deaf people is never direct.*